HEADING HOME

GROWING UP IN BASEBALL

HEADING HOME

GROWING UP IN BASEBALL

PHOTOGRAPHS BY
HARRY CONNOLLY

FOREWORD BY
CAL RIPKEN, JR.

INTRODUCTION BY
STEPHEN KING

Rizzoli
NEW YORK

First published in the
United States of America in 1995
by RIZZOLI INTERNATIONAL
PUBLICATIONS, INC.
300 Park Avenue South,
New York, NY 10010

Library of Congress
Cataloging-in-Publication Data

Connolly, Harry.
Heading home: growing up in
baseball / by Harry Connolly ;
foreword by Cal Ripken, Jr. ;
introduction by Stephen King.
p.   cm.
ISBN 0-8478-1889-6
1. Baseball for Children—Pictorial
works. I. Title.
GV880.5.C65 1995   94-47357
796.357'62—dc20   CIP

Designed by Alex Castro

Printed and bound in Singapore

For Renée with love
Season after season she listens to my stories,
looks at my pictures, keeps the faith.

ACKNOWLEDGMENTS

Chuck Verrill is the reason this book exists.
My thanks to Chuck, Liz Darhansoff, and
Leigh Feldman for their friendship and counsel.
Thanks to Stephen King and Cal Ripken, Jr.,
for their double-play contribution. To Manuela
Soares, my wonderful editor, and Alex Castro,
the designer, for making it both better and fun.
To Tom Wilson, Bruce McCall, and Daniel
Okrent for pointing me in the right direction.
To Jon Buck, aviator, for flying me over the
park. Thanks to Mike Feinstein, Rob Szabo,
Walter Gomez and the Gomez Gallery, Ron
Shapiro, JoAnn Peroutka, Stephen Doyle,
Service Photo, Jacqueline Watts, The East
Baltimore Guide, Don Scott, Marty Bass,
and Bruce Springsteen.
      Affectionate thanks to my home team:
Renée, Wil, and Joey. And to my sisters:
Marion, Caroline, Anne, Eileen, and Rosemary.
      To run a baseball league for kids requires
time, money, and dedication. Special thanks to
Joe Bormel, Buck Gough, Ron Wiley, and The
Exchange Club of Highlandtown, Inc. Thanks
also to the coaches and parents who have
helped over the years, especially Tim Monath,
Rick Sebastian, Dave Good, Bill Warfield,
Sharon Costello, and Mary Cox.
      The boys and girls of Patterson Park let
me into their world, showed me what matters,
changed everything. Thanks, kids.

Preface

HARRY CONNOLLY

IN THE HEART OF EAST BALTIMORE, surrounded by well-kept row houses, churches, schools, and a few bars, Patterson Park is a destination for young and old. Children cross busy streets and find themselves surrounded by green, free to play, to goof off, to be kids. This park has much to offer: playgrounds, tennis courts, swimming pools, jungle gyms, biking and jogging trails, soccer fields, and even a small stadium. What it gave me was the William H. Schultz Fields, two side-by-side baseball fields where, over the span of six summers, I photographed children playing baseball.

Standing on those fields, I felt as though I was in the middle of a grand American theater piece. The playing fields and fences formed the stage; trees and row houses provided the backdrop. On these fields, Al Kaline and Reggie Jackson once played. Today the players are kids named Wilbur, Shane, Martha, Josh, Becky, and Mario, with nicknames like Scooter, "Allright" Albright, Dizzy, Daffy, Egghead, (Grass) 'Stain, Ice Man, Short Stuff, Opie, Tweedledee, Skeeter, and Homer. These are American faces playing the American game. Their props are baseballs, bats, and gloves; uniforms and summer clothes are their costumes.

I was a stranger to the neighborhood when I began my work. On my knees, I began to photograph the children. Their parents looked at me with suspicion, but when I returned with small prints for the kids, which they treated as baseball cards, that broke the ice. To the kids I became

"Mr. Harry," and even the parents opened up to me. The photographs from that first summer show only children—rough-and-tumble kids playing baseball on two fields in a city park. Every game was different, the expected rarely happened, and being there was usually a blast. The kids and I saw the park as a place of play, promise, and possibilities. Here I might show baseball's beginnings, its significance to one neighborhood, and have fun doing so.

Each season began on a cool April day and ended on a warm July evening. I photographed the park from an airplane, the field from a ladder, and the kids from whatever angle that worked. On these fields, 8- to 10- and 10- to 12-year-olds play. Their team names are borrowed from the big leagues: Expos, Cardinals, Red and White Sox, Mets, Dodgers, A's, and, of course, the hometown Orioles. Local realtors, restaurants, law firms, oil companies, and stores serve as sponsors and their names appear prominently on the team jerseys. The audience is composed mostly of family and friends, all interested in the outcome. Wins and losses are noted, all-stars chosen, champions crowned; values are taught, lessons learned, and traditions continued.

Games are played evenings and Saturdays. As the summers went by, people realized that I was genuinely interested in them and their relationships to each other, to their neighborhood, to the game of baseball. They began asking me to photograph them! That request was never turned down. I photographed the children with their families, friends, teammates, and the occasional pet. I followed them on and off the field, before and after the game—hitting, catching, winning, losing, getting hurt, having fun. Some children, like Richard (cover), I photographed for a year or two and then never saw again. Others, like Dominic (page 38) and Josh (page 42), I watched grow and develop into good players.

Just as the children learned a few lessons over these summers, so did I. I saw that some stories took time to tell and that the passage of time can be an asset. I learned to relax and become friends with many of the people pictured here. My photograph of Wilbur (page 125) has made him a local celebrity. Newspapers and magazines have written about him. He has appeared on local TV. People ask him for his autograph. His grandmother can't thank me enough for being there to take that picture. When I stopped by Dominic's house one day with some new pictures, his

mother showed me a small album tied with a pink ribbon. Inside were all the small contact prints I had taken of her sons over the years. Along the way a balance had been struck. This park and these people mean a great deal to me, and my photographs matter to them.

From the air you can see that these fields are cut out of the park, and that the park could easily reclaim them. But children have been playing baseball games here for over forty years with no end in sight. By playing the game, standing at the plate, running the bases, these children reinforce the diamond's design that keeps the game and their neighborhood alive. In some small way, I hope that my photographs do the same.

Foreword

CAL RIPKEN, JR.

WHEN I THINK BACK TO MY LITTLE LEAGUE DAYS I visualize how special the game was when I first discovered it—the feeling it gave me on my early successes. There is an old saying in baseball when things aren't going well—"you must return to the basics"—the simplicity of hitting, throwing, and fielding. This refers only to the physical and fundamental aspects of returning to the basics, but I've learned to take this one step farther. For me, the mental side, being able to reflect back to the era defined in Harry Connolly's photographs, gives me the energy to deal with anything professional baseball can dish out.

As I was leafing through these photographs, I felt as though I was returning to a special place in my own childhood. These shots were not of me or my Little League teammates, but they made me feel and remember as if they were. This book captures the pure essence of baseball that is common to us all. We all couldn't go on to be major league players. The fact of the matter is, as you get older and baseball gets more competitive, fewer people get the chance to play. Having experienced every possible phase of baseball as a player and having grown up in a professional baseball atmosphere, I'm very aware of how the game of baseball and how it is approached changes as you get better and continue to play. Winning and success become all important. That's not bad,

but with this come certain pressures. When the pressures have gotten a little unbearable I've always taken comfort in remembering the times when the games were played for the pure joy of it. When, for this brief phase in my life, the playing field was level and everyone was equal.

I remember vividly when I played my first game on an actual baseball diamond. It was a huge lot behind a school along with several other baseball fields. I thought it was the best field on the planet. The grass was freshly cut, the dirt was smooth, the chalk lines were straight as an arrow, and we had actual bases. There were no fences and there really wasn't a mound, but that didn't matter. It seemed so glamorous then! If you looked closely now, here's what you'd find: grass that is freshly cut but only partly finished, dirt not so smooth mixed with a few rocks, and chalk lines that are wavy at best. But that's the true flavor of kid's baseball—a game to play, a place to play it, and a little imagination.

Unless you were a coach, of course, and then you needed a lot of imagination. For the most part, the coaches were volunteer fathers. My relationships with coaches were different than most kids because I was knowledgeable about baseball at an early age. In some cases, I knew more than the coaches. It wasn't uncommon for me to be used as a baseball resource: How does your dad teach you to hold a bat? How does he take batting practice? What's the proper way to hold a baseball? The thing I remember the most about the coaches was their gift of time. Without them there wouldn't be any games. They brought the equipment, lined the fields, installed the bases, and made sure everyone got to play.

The teams were made up of different kinds of kids with different kinds of backgrounds. Some kids had the best gloves and the best cleats, some didn't even have a glove. Some had their parents drive them to every game, some had to miss games for lack of a ride. There were kids from private schools and kids from public schools. We found out that

Cal, number 22, and his
National League team.

there were many differences in each other, but the one similarity was
the only thing we cared about—baseball.

Friendship was a big part of Little League. Friendships were especially important to me when I played Little League in North Carolina. My
dad managed the Asheville Orioles for the summers of 1972 through
1974 and he enrolled me in a Little League program in West Asheville.
Moving to Asheville for the summer was a big adjustment for our family,
because we were leaving all of our friends behind and going to a place
where we didn't know anyone. Little League was the way I was able to
make new friends. We were all joined together by at least one common

interest, baseball. I found that I had a lot of other things in common with some of my teammates and good friendships were made.

When I played in North Carolina, we went to the regional play-offs of the Little League World Series in St. Petersburg, Florida. There was a one game elimination, which made it highly stressful, full of pressure—one game and you're out of the tournament. We ultimately ended up losing to a team from Kentucky. We all bawled our eyes out. I was the losing pitcher and I felt responsibile for not getting us to the National Tournament in Williamsport. After the game, everybody on the team blamed themselves for things they thought they did wrong. The home run I gave up ended up right at the fence and the left fielder thought he should have caught it. Though we all were disappointed, the whole experience was still fun and exhilarating. The team got to travel as a group and we enjoyed a lot of successes together.

Little League was a time when we could try anything and everything. We had no idea what our limits were or anyone else's. The game was new and fresh to explore. This was a time when we found out what batting stance we liked. We copied the big leaguers—Brooks Robinson, Frank Robinson, Pete Rose, Johnny Bench, Joe Morgan, and Tony Perez—we copied our dad, our coach, anyone we saw and that was okay. We found out about the whole game basically the same way—observation, trial, and a lot of errors. There were certain fundamentals we learned and applied, but we had the freedom, based on our abilities and talent, to experiment. I

Photo / Violet Ripken

Cal (center) in 1972 as a member of the Asheville All Stars the year they played in the regional championships.

played shortstop, I pitched, and I tried to be a catcher for a while because that was the position my dad had played. Catching is where the action is, and I'm sure my dad took a lot of pride in the fact that I was playing his position, but I didn't like putting on the gear and getting back there and stooping down. I just didn't enjoy it as much as the other positions.

We were essentially discovering the game itself and how we could play it. In the process, we learned a lot about ourselves, too. Of course, we weren't alone in these revelations. Besides the teammates and coaches there were fans, which, in Little League, means your family—with the occasional best friend or girl friend stopping by. Some parents, I'm sure, viewed these events as social gatherings, where the grown-ups could engage in a little adult conversation and the younger kids could get together for a larger play group, testing their skills on foreign monkey bars and swing sets. I think of these families as the "social" group, generally laid back, enjoying the game and the whole family atmosphere. Then there was the "serious" group, much more intense. They would be the ones rooting at the top of their lungs, yelling at the umpires, and keeping track of every statistic (probably for bragging rights).

My family fell somewhere in the middle. My mom came to every one of my games in place of my father, who usually couldn't come because his season as a professional baseball coach coincided with my Little League career. When he had an occasional day off he would come see me play. I was always a little nervous when my dad was there. I tried extra hard to do well. I wanted to show him how good I was and make him proud of me. I don't remember having my best games when he was there and that taught me an important lesson about myself: the harder I try, the more I try to do, the less I seem to accomplish. My secret is to try hard, but to have fun. I don't try to do more than I'm capable of doing. It's important for me to relax and just be myself.

Since my dad wasn't at most of my games, I had to fill him in on everything that happened. Talking to him about my games helped us develop a pretty good relationship. He would always listen and he always seemed to have a solution to any problems I might be having. It seemed he often knew what had happened without even being there and seeing it.

In the beginning of the season, it was common to see my mother in her lawn chair by herself, away from the team bench and the bleachers full of other parents. I didn't know exactly why she sat there, but it made me feel great to know she was watching. Later I came to understand that she separated herself for two reasons: She didn't believe in the pressures and seriousness invoked by some of the parents and coaches; and she wanted me to know she was there for me. She never openly preached this philosophy, but it was amazing how contagious it became. By the end of the season I'd look over to see that my mom had her own lawn chair fan club.

While there wasn't intense pressure in Little League, all of us had our share of disappointments. Just because I became a major leaguer doesn't make me exempt; I had my share. I've made the last out of the game, made errors that cost the game, lost my control pitching and had to be taken out. These are real disappointments, especially at an early age. My family was there to offer comfort. On some of those long walks from the field to the car, my mother would say things like "You'll get 'em next time," or "You can't have a good day every day." It doesn't seem like much, but when your mother or father says it you know somehow that everything will be fine. And by the time I would get to the car everything was fine.

The only advice my dad ever gave me about Little League was to have fun. My advice to kids playing in any kid's league today would be to have fun, try all of the positions to find out which one you like the best, learn all of the rules—because it adds to the fun, and to be a good teammate and friend.

As a professional baseball player, without a doubt, Little League helped shape my life. I also believe that the experience of Little League has helped shape the lives of everybody who has ever played it. In the Major Leagues, even though we're from all parts of the country, we often sit around and talk about our Little League memories. Baseball is our common ground. It all started somewhere and usually, you can trace it back to kid's league play.

We can all identify with the photographs in this book, imagining what made those kids laugh or if they made the catch after the picture was snapped. We can all remember how we learned to handle the competition, challenges, and discoveries we made during those summers, lessons that effect how we live as adults, faced with new forms of competition and challenge. Whatever Little League was to each of us individually, I feel certain we can all say that it was a very special time. It was more than just playing the game. It gave us the freedom to try, it was a chance for family togetherness, and a time to make new friendships. Harry's photos conjure up clear and concise images and very special memories from the times I spent in the parks, behind the schools, and on the fields where kid's league games were played.

Introduction

STEPHEN KING

IN 1989, I WAS PART-TIME COACH and full-time scorekeeper for the Little League All-Star team from my home town, which went on to win the State Championship that year. I was also at various times groundskeeper, linesman, and equipment manager; as every parent who's ever volunteered for a youth league knows, you quickly learn to become a utility player. If you want to keep your sanity, that is.

As is the case with most parents, I got involved because my son was on the team. But before the season ended, I got to know all the boys, to love some of them, to realize I'd been a fool to ever drift away from youth baseball, and to be intensely grateful that God or Fate or Whatever had given me a second chance. I've been involved ever since, and expect to be for a long time to come.

I've kept rough track of the Boys of '89—partially because I wrote about them in a long essay called "Head Down," partially because my son was one of them and has continued to play various sports with many of them, and partially out of the simple curiosity that seems to be part of a writer's basic equipment package—an almost unassuageable urge to know how the story comes out.

There were fourteen kids on the team which won the State Championship in '89, a squad culled from the hundred and ten kids or so who showed up for All-Star tryouts. Roger Fisher, who started the Final

for our guys, moved to Las Vegas with his family in the fall of that year, and has disappeared from my ken. The other thirteen are still around, but the four years between '89, when most of them were twelve, and '93, when most are sixteen and juniors in high school, have brought a lot of changes. Some haven't been exactly wonderful. Coaches and poets have very few overlapping belief systems, but on one subject both would tell you the same thing: time is rarely the friend of young athletes.

Only six of the thirteen boys who were on our All-Star team in the summer of '89 played high school varsity or junior varsity baseball in the spring of '93. Some of the other seven were cut after tryouts; others, knowing it is usually easier on the ego to quit than wait to get fired, simply stayed away from tryouts altogether. Easier to concentrate on dramatics, debate, or,

28

in the case of Kevin Rochefort, who played third base for the '89 team, Varsity Golf. There's not a thing wrong with debate or dramatics or golf, of course, and I don't mean to imply that there is, but every time I pick up my son's yearbook and see that picture of Kevin with a putter instead of an infielder's mitt, I hear the hiss of Time the Avenger's scythe and have to restrain an urge to lace my hands over the nape of my neck and duck.

So there were fourteen little Indians…and then there were thirteen…and then there were six. And when college baseball tryouts start in February of 1996, I suspect there will be only two left from the original group. My son will be using his big first baseman's mitt only in pick-up games by then, and that's perfectly okay by me. In some ways, it will be a relief.

For now my point is just this: There are few places in American society where the Darwinian creed of natural selection is allowed to work itself from first to last with so little tinkering, tampering, or interference as in sports. Each sport is a pyramid, with the pros at the top (and the crème de la crème—people like Michael Jordan, Bobby Orr, and Barry Bonds standing on the shoulders of the rank-and-file) and the lowliest amateurs—the kids—sprawling out at the bottom. With each passing year and each ascending level, the surface area gets smaller and more people drop away. As you look through the photographs that follow— the wonderful photographs that follow—you should keep in mind that the odds against any of these children ever playing baseball for money (or even at the College World Series in Omaha) are astronomical.

But that is maybe not so bad, and that's why I'm losing zero sleep over the fact that my son, Owen, is probably never going to play first base for a college team. I've been following youth sports for a long time, and I'm not sure the game is worth the candle. Every time a kid makes it to the next level of the pyramid, the price goes up. The further you go, the harder you have to work. There's the constant conditioning that has to be done. There's the pain of muscles which are routinely pushed to peak effort—

and then beyond. There's the mental and spiritual toll exacted by having to perform at stress levels which are sometimes in the yellow caution zone, and sometimes well past the redline.

Sometimes the engine can take that kind of pounding; sometimes it throws a rod or blows wide open. Think of the stories you have read about college athletes in trouble with drugs, money, or both; think about pro athletes who are hounded by the media when they do well and excoriated by both fans and the press when they fail—as even the best athletes in pro sports do three times out of every five. Nor are these prices exacted just at the pro and college levels; would that they were. If you don't believe that many high school jocks live in the same pressure-cooker, I suggest you read *Friday Night Lights*, H.G. Bissinger's terrifying dissection of high school football in Texas.

You see it in their eyes, sometimes—pros like Jose Canseco and Rickey Henderson, who know they can do nothing or say nothing that will please the press—and sometimes you see it in their actions: the fighter who trashes his car in a fit of anger, the football player who suddenly wheels and hucks his helmet at an assistant coach, a baseball player overturning a batrack and scattering the lumber everywhere.

Go to a high school basketball tourney and you will see high school girls and boys playing with clamped jaws and desperate, intent eyes—as if their lives, and the lives of their loved ones, depended on the outcome of what was once nothing but a Saturday afternoon pastime played with no fans and no officials, played not for fame or acclaim—let alone money—but simply for joy. And joy, I think, is what most of these photographs are about, and why they hit my head and heart like a drink of cool water on a hot day. They are pictures of people who have not yet heard of Time the Avenger, kids who have no idea of how painful it can be to creep up to a list posted on the door of a high school or junior high school athletic office—and see that your name is not on it.

Harry Connolly's exuberant, joyful pictures of kid's league baseball express how wonderful life can be on the first layer of the sports pyramid. There, miracle of miracles, everyone is allowed to stand and there's still plenty of room to breathe and you don't have a worry in the world about being jostled off one of the sides. I looked slowly through these images, which are generous and open and filled with a kind of bright naturalism, and was all but overwhelmed by the conviction that this is the way it's supposed to be. If I needed a reaffirmation of my decision to be involved with youth baseball, all it would take is a look at the picture of the Fred Gross/Marex White Sox, lined up against the chain-link fence of their dugout. All eight of the kids in the picture are smiling, not one of the smiles looks forced or faked, and there is nothing tense or guarded about their eyes—they are the eyes of kids who are having fun (and in the case of the pipsqueak, third from the right, they are the eyes of a kid who is having the absolute time of his life).

There is also a baseball glove in this picture, but it's so far in the foreground that it's out of focus. It's the kids who are in focus, not the glove, and in a way that says everything that needs to be said about kids and baseball. You may make baskets of money in the bigs, and you may get to go steady with a cheerleader in the middles, but in the littles, my friend, you have a natural blast. Just ask the kids of Fred Gross/Marex if you don't believe me, or the kids from the Bormel Realty A's. These kids are stylin'. They're livin' it large.

The game is still allowed to make them happy. These are the faces of children who have not yet been told that the dream is usually just on loan, there to be looked at and lived in and enjoyed only for a short, golden time—the years when you come back from the field, sit on the back step, and pour the sand out of your sneakers before going in barefoot to eat your supper. The dream is usually on loan, and you are not allowed to leave the building with it. What building? Why childhood, silly. That building. Around the time the first pimples start to show up on your cheeks and forehead, they take the bright, shiny dream out of your hands, put it back on the shelf for the next kid to enjoy—and shoo you on out the door.

These are pictures of the dreams which exist in childhood, and for me that makes them pieces of working magic—a magic that exists within the unguileful eyes and unguarded expressions of kids who have not yet discovered the necessity for believing that the idea of magic is a lie. It will still be a year or two before some coach tells those chasing the dream across the fields of middle school and toward those of high school to get on their game faces. This is an age when it's still okay to cry if you strike out to end the game, or to scream deliriously if you drive one over the center fielder's head to get your first hit of the season (after striking out fourteen times and being hit twice by fastballs, once in The Place Where It Really Hurts). When you're still just a member of the State Farm Red Sox, playing Farm League ball and hitting off a tee—at least at the start of the season—it is still acceptable to try and field grounders with your eyes shut (there's an amazing, wonderful picture of just that in this book). And no coach is yet cruel enough to walk up to you while you're on the ground, writhing in pain, and tell you to Shake It Off.

A couple of other things deserve to be mentioned. One is that youth baseball programs may be the last time that kids are totally unselfconscious about having their parents at their games, watching and cheering them on. If you have a boy or girl playing ball at this level—seven to fourteen, let's say—you probably know what I'm talking about. If you don't, I ask you to study the photographs of parents and children which follow with particular care. I also ask you to remember that sound I mentioned—the whisper of the scythe—and to keep in mind the fact that you will be hearing it yourself, soon enough. The time your children spend playing on these dusty, nonchalant little fields behind schools and bottling plants and housing developments is going to be all too short. Hold it while you have it—that's my advice.

There are pictures of kids with their dads here, but I think the ones I like the best are those of mothers and sons. I have looked again and again at the picture of the woman wearing the tee-shirt that says My Stepmother Is An Alien, her arm around her son's shoulder, both of them comfortable in their closeness (if a little suspicious of the photographer), and the picture of the stocky black kid, cheerfully surrounded by his mother's prodigious forearms. The love of these parents and children is as confident and open as their attitude about the game. Someone will eventually tell these kids—one blonde and fair and skinny, the other black-haired, brown-skinned, and chunky—that it's not cool to get your picture taken with your momma. Hopefully they won't listen, but a lot of them do. Yes indeed, a lot of them do.

The second thing I want to point out is that there is a pleasant self-referential quality to these photos. They all seem to have been taken at a single field, but they go beyond expressing a feeling of community; it's almost as if they are offering us intersecting views of another world, one which overlaps our own but is not precisely of our own.

I would argue that that's pretty much what baseball is at this level, and that it is also the genius of these photographs. Silently, persuasively, Harry Connolly offers us an emotional landscape where there is shade but few real shadows, winners but no real losers, weirdos but no real outsiders. These are fields where little sisters are still tolerated and where excellence is hoped for and appreciated, but never expected. It is a magic place because it is one of the few where adult organization and childhood play are still in balance. Connolly's photographs reflect this world beautifully, achieving their own balance between clarity and mystery and holding our eye through an entire cycle of images. In this world dreams are still clear (if sometimes grimy), often round, and held with the fingers over the seams. The poetic fragility and prosaic reality of kids at play has rarely been expressed as well as they are here, in these beautiful black and white images.

Kids in the Small Fry League await their coach's instructions after lining up for some practice catching in the outfield.

IT BEGINS IN EARLY SPRING. Children sign up to play and are assigned a league based on their age. The Small Fry (seen here) are 5 to 7 years old. At this level, the children first try to figure out which hand their glove goes on. Then they must learn to put fear aside and attempt to catch the ball as it hurtles toward them.

For now, there is time to practice before they are expected to play in a real game. Time to watch the coaches and the other kids and to try and figure out what to do next.

The only thing that feels right is their baseball cap; the only thing that comes easy is daydreaming. Constantly, they are told to pay attention. But the game, the other kids, are all too new; there are just too many distractions. This time next year, they will have learned some lessons, how to catch, how to hit, maybe even how to pay attention in the outfield.

Dominic at age 4 (left), and hitting with a lot more confidence (above) just a few years later at age 7.

Cousins Dominic and Chris, ages 3 and 7. Dominic was too young to play and could barely hold the baseball even with both hands. He often watched Chris play in the Small Fry League.

Dominic and Chris posed again four years later, ages 7 and 11. This time they were both playing ball—Chris in the National League for children 10 to 12 and Dominic in the International League for children 8 to 10.

Josh as a Small Fry (left) and making a play in the outfield four years later (right). He has been an All-Star in each league.

In early spring,
a newcomer tries to
put the bat to the ball.

AT EVERY LEVEL, the basics are taught. The coaches get down in the grass with the Small Fry, showing them how it all works, taking them step-by-step through the basics of the game, holding the ball, throwing the ball, catching the ball.

When teaching them how to hit the ball, the coach stands behind each child and wraps his arms around theirs. He shows them how to place their hands on the bat and the proper way to swing. The kids practice hitting the ball as it sits on a plastic tee. The ball can sit there, untouched, for a very long time.

After a while, with enough practice, some of these skills will be learned and used in a game. For kids in Small Fry, it is still a game of mistakes, but occasionally the ball will be hit and caught; a play will be made, a run will score. It's a start.

Coach Kenny instructs the Small
Fry (left). Learning how to hold a
bat for the first time can take a
lot of effort (right).

(Left) Catching one ball is hard enough. (Right) Success sometimes comes as a surprise.

49

Hitting and catching aren't as easy as they look. Luckily for this young player (right), the Small Fry use a ball that is regulation size, but softer than the standard baseball.

Off the field, Small Fry Jackie loved to ham it up for the camera.

After a messy trip to the water fountain, this young man was determined to be photographed just like this.

The International League
Orioles in uniform (left).
(Right) Waiting for the ball
or just blocking the sun?

Having moved into the next league, for 8- to 10- year-olds, these boys are a bit older, more experienced at the game, and it shows.

Superboy practiced occasionally with the local kids one summer, but he was gone—after just one season.

Rebekah is a dedicated player and comes from a baseball family. Her brother Josh (page 42) and sister Jackie (page 50) play, too. Both her parents are involved in the Highland-town League, her father is an umpire and coach, and her mother is an assistant coach and scorekeeper.

In the International League, the kids suddenly begin to look like the big league ballplayers they all admire. Having learned the basics, maybe they're enjoying the game more, too.

Between games, it's practice time. The kids get together
and practice several times a week during the season.

Some kids are better at this sport than others. Sometimes you can see it in their eyes, or the way they hold the bat. And sometimes, all they have to do is just stand there.

Heather and one of her coaches share a moment during a game (left). Coach Wayne Turner and his son, Craig (right).

GAME TIME IS FAMILY TIME. Parents come to watch their children play ball. Some will have kids playing on both fields and they must stand behind the screen that separates them so they can watch both games at the same time. Brothers, sisters, and cousins may find themselves on the same team or they can be on opposite sides.

On the sidelines, people sit on blankets, in lawn chairs, on the grass. Kids play games, ride bikes, eat hot dogs, drink sodas. Dogs run loose. Most of the family moments take place after the game, but parents and children, coaches and players also pitch in to prepare the field before each game and share a few moments together. There is a great deal of pride and love here.

Every boy and girl should be lucky enough to have a mother's love
or a father's embrace like the ones you see on these pages.

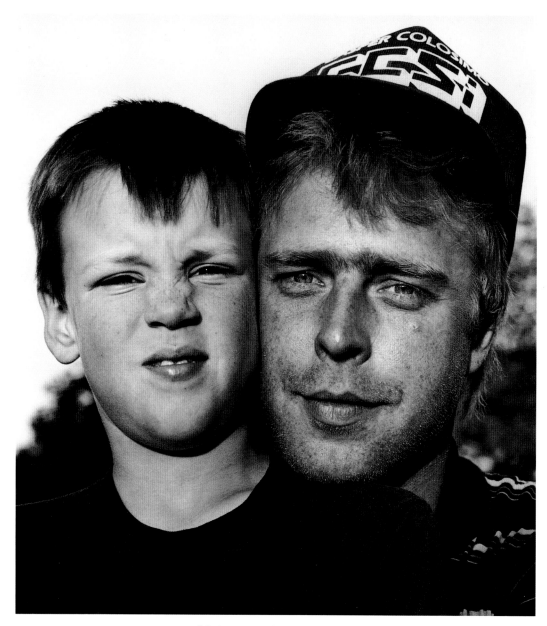

Not all fathers can make it to the games, but the pride is evident when they do.

Three generations often
spend the afternoon together
at the baseball field (right).

Four-legged family members are frequent, and
sometimes disruptive, visitors to the games.

Nine-year-old Martha (left) shares a moment with her cousin. Mother and daughter (above) take in a game.

Small Fry Ryan, new to the game, has a protective arm around his sister Holly (left). Holly and Ryan just a few years later (right).

From International League to National League, Matt and his mother in pictures taken three years apart.

Mothers and sons.

Mr. Crowe coached for a year or two during his son's career as an International League Red Sox.

"Mr. Lou" is a park fixture, having coached here for many years.

Coach Steve Malczewski is joined by his two sons, Matt (left) and Chris, and a teammate (right), as he hammers in the pitching rubber. Two coaches arrive with the equipment (right).

BEFORE EACH GAME, the coaches mark off the baselines, hammer in the bases, and check the field conditions. These conditions depend on two mysterious forces: the City of Baltimore and Mother Nature. So the grass is cut when the grass is cut and watered whenever it rains. One very dry summer, someone dropped a lit cigarette and set the outfield on fire. It was quickly extinguished and the game went on.

It's a six-inning game. Every kid must play for three innings and have one at bat. Each team has fifteen kids, with ten kids playing. At the Small Fry level, there are lots of outfielders, though the ball doesn't usually get past second base. In the International League, there are four outfielders, but the National League uses only three, just like the big leagues.

The rules are simple; the game is complicated. The pitcher cannot throw the ball over the plate. There are a lot of walks; any batter who reaches first base will likely score, helped along by more walks, wild pitches, passed balls, fielder's errors. If the batter can put the ball in play, chances are good he will reach first base. If he can get the ball to the outfield, a home run is likely. Every play is an adventure; every good play a pleasant and often stunning surprise.

First the wind-up, and then, the pitch.

Below: Wild pitches are a regular, and expected, occurrence. Following pages: A National League Cardinal works on his swing with some phantom hitting in the on-deck circle (left).
National League catcher Homer (right) is a formidable presence behind the plate.

Action in the outfield as the catch is made!

At the plate, the catcher tries to throw out a runner attempting to steal second base.

Standing on third base hoping to score (left). The umpire calls a strike (right). Most games are close, but there are high scoring games: 34 to 26, a four inning game called on account of darkness, and 54 to 1, another four inning game called as an act of kindness.

The outfield begins to look a little crowded as four players rush to make the play.

Sometimes the ball is caught.

Amazingly enough, this ball was finally caught (right).

And sometimes it's not.

A collision in the outfield (right), not an uncommon occurence, allows a player to reach base (left).

A coach consoles one of his players after a
tough loss.

A post-game conference between players and coaches ends a game (right). Derek (below) helps put some of the equipment away after a game.

After-the-game high jinks for Mario.

Carl, the catcher, looking fierce.

After all of the excitement of the game, kids let off steam by lapping the bases, sliding into home plate, and kicking up the dirt.

Taking a break from All-Star practice.

THIS IS HOW IT BEGAN. One Friday evening in May, I thought I would head down to the park and see what I could find. On the field were kids, high-spirited, wisecracking 8- to 10-year-olds, playing a pretty good game. They were casually dressed; what gave them away were their team hats. These were the All-Stars, selected by their coaches, getting ready for tomorrow's game.

I walked onto the field and started taking pictures. At first the kids acted as if they didn't care but soon they were mugging for the camera, striking slugger poses, crossing bats, having fun. The late afternoon light cast long shadows which disappeared as the sun set. The kids played on. I stayed. Something told me that I was in the right place and that portraits would be the heart of it all. Some of the faces speak very much about today; others look as if they were photographed many years ago. Many of the kids are wide-eyed and open to the world; for others life has not been so easy.

The faces that follow are some of my National League All-Stars.

113

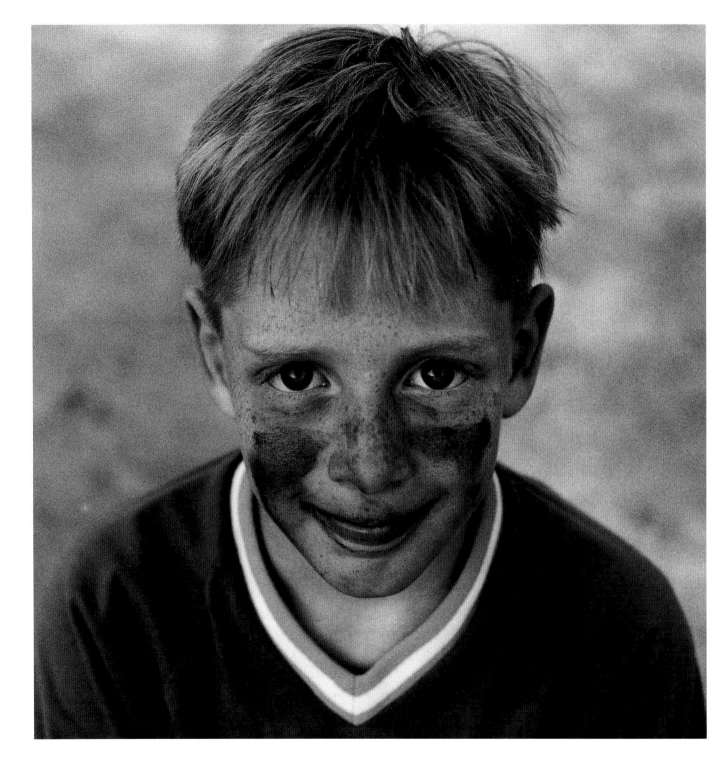

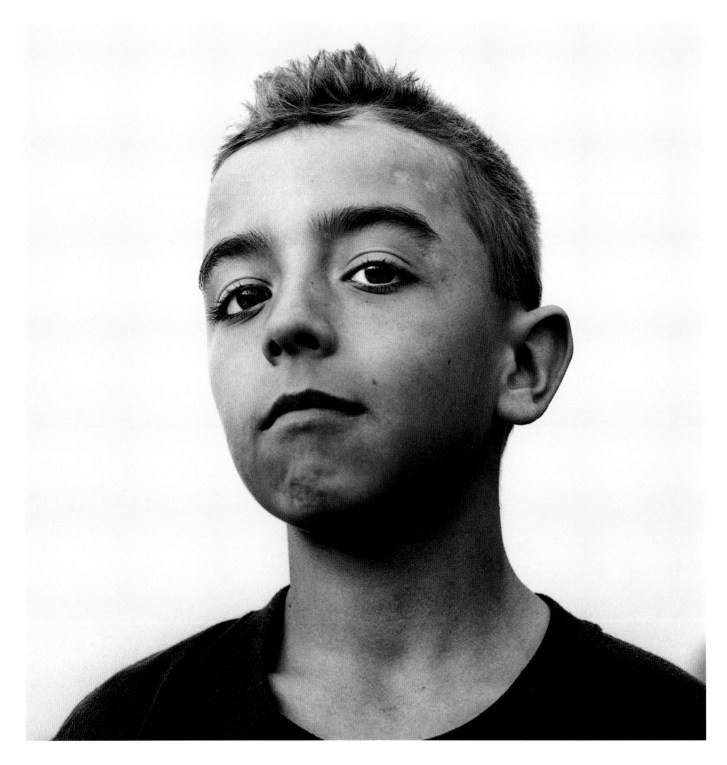

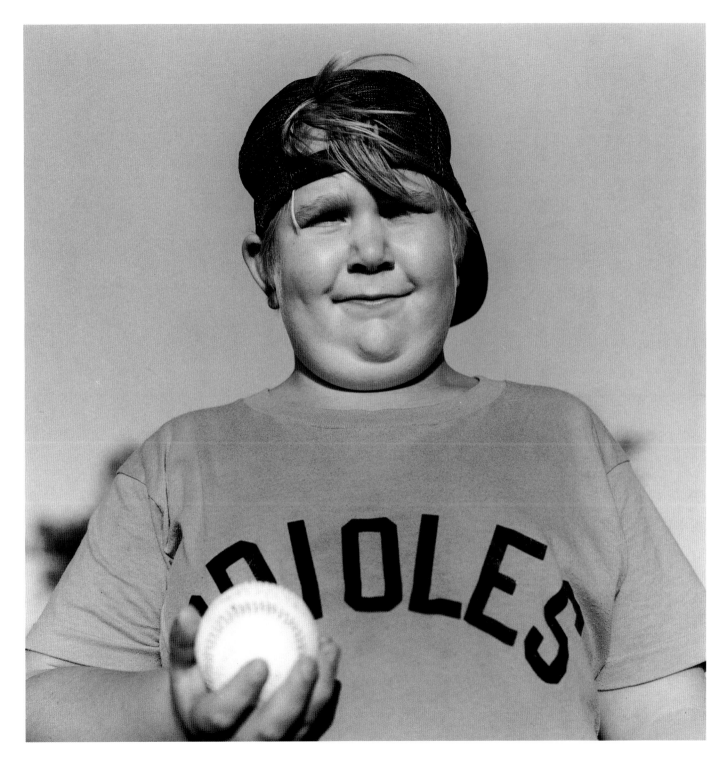

Everyone on the winning team,
including the coaches, gets a trophy in
the International League championships.

TO A KID, WINNING IS NICE, but not that
important; losing matters even less. What
matters is the hit, the catch, crossing
home plate, having fun. To stand on the
bench with your teammates, hats on
inside out, rally cap–style chanting: H-O,
H-O-M, H-O-M-E-R-U-N as your teammate heads to the plate with the bases
loaded; to look around and see family and
friends cheering you on—that's what this
is all about. But one team has to win it all:
the game, the championship, the small
bragging rights, the trophy. The season
will soon be over.

Just like the big leaguers, using two bats to warm-up (left). In his own world (right), a hitter prepares for his turn at bat.

There are fewer mistakes and a lot more intensity in championship games. The level of play is better, but the kids don't seem to have any less fun.

With a player on first base (left), there has to be a conference on the mound (above). The batter waits for his pitch (right).

A player rounds third base on his way home (left), as the ball continues into the outfield (right).

After the game, the players, winners and losers, exchange the ritual "high-fives." And then it's time to celebrate (next page).

As hats fly high into the air (right), the coach (below) must crouch for his victory shower.

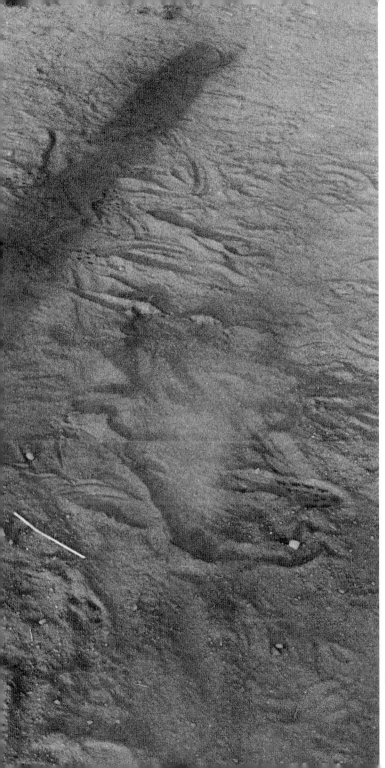

THERE WILL BE ONE MORE GAME: the children versus their parents and coaches. Guess who wins? For the rest of the summer, kids will use these fields in a less organized way. They will play pick-up games, making up the rules as they go. They will play some ball, pretend they are Cal Ripken or Ken Griffey, Jr., razz one another, race around the bases, dive into the grass, play in the dirt. At the end of the day, when it is hard to see that dirty white ball, they will make plans for tomorrow. As the street lights come on, they will gather up their gloves, bats, and balls, get one last drink from the water fountain, and leave the park. Time to be heading home.

Say, hey!

155

Editor's Note

Baseball is played all across America — in sandlots and stadiums, backyards and ball parks. It's a game that seems to transcend age, ethnicity, gender, and culture.

Baseball is available to boys and girls of all ages in many forms — neighborhood games in the park, and more organized endeavors in locally formed teams and leagues, some affiliated with Little League Baseball, Incorporated, or with other organizations. In the organized local leagues, baseball often becomes a family affair with parents taking on the roles of coach, umpire, and scorekeeper.

This book is based on the League that organizes baseball for children in Baltimore, Maryland. In this way, it reflects the many groups across the country where parents and children share their love for the national sport. While the introductory essays by Stephen King and Cal Ripken, Jr., describe their own experiences with teams affiliated with the Little League® Baseball organization, this book has no connection to the Little League® organization and is not meant to be a book about official Little League® activities.